she DARED

— BETHANY HAMILTON —

Also by Jenni L. Walsh

SHE DARED: MALALA YOUSAFZAI

she

DARED

— BETHANY HAMILTON —

JENNI L. WALSH

Scholastic Inc.

While this book is a work of nonfiction, a few literary elements, such as
brief dialogue, have been imagined by the author in order to make the
narrative more relatable and immediate.

UNAUTHORIZED.
This book is not sponsored, approved, or endorsed by anyone who
appears in this book.

ISBN 978-1-338-14902-9

10 9 8 7 6 5 4 3 2   19 20 21 22 23

Printed in the U.S.A.   40

First edition, January 2019

Book design by Maeve Norton

Photos ©: cover: AFP/Getty Images; back cover: Kirstin
Scholtz/ZUMAPress/Newscom; 1 top: D.Fujimoto/The Garden Island/
ZUMAPress/Newscom; 1 bottom: Pierre Leclerc/Shutterstock; 2 top:
Yoshinori/Shutterstock; 2 bottom: Sport the Library SportsChrome/
Newscom; 3: The AGE/Getty Images; 4 top: Allen J. Schaben/Getty
Images; 4 bottom: Kevin Winter/Getty Images; 5 top: Toby Canham/
Splash News/Newscom; 5 bottom: Icon Sports Wire/Getty Images; 6 top:
Edward Ajaj Feature Photo Service/Newscom; 6 bottom: Kirstin Scholtz/
ZUMAPress/Newscom; 7 top: CBS Photo Archive/Getty Images;
7 bottom: Mike Neal; 8: Nick Agro/AP Images.

For fearless kiddos
everywhere, especially
Kaylee and Devlin

CHAPTER 1

FOURTEEN-FOOT TIGER SHARK

A red surfboard, acting as a street sign, stuck out of the ground. It was marked with the word *Tunnels*. As in Tunnels Beach. As in Bethany Hamilton's last attempt to find a surfing spot with decent waves that morning. Her mom maneuvered Blue Crush—their ancient 1988 Dodge Caravan—into the parking lot. Bethany put her empty cereal bowl aside and hopped out, for the third time that October morning. She jogged in the glow of their van's headlights toward the beach to survey the surf conditions.

Glassy. Flat. Not great for surfing. Just like the other surf spots they had checked over the last hour.

Bethany had gotten up at 5:00 a.m. on a holiday and ate breakfast on the go for this?

Okay, maybe that holiday was Halloween and not that big a deal. Christmas was her favorite holiday anyway. Her family would wake up early to surf, when everyone else was opening presents. A thirteen-year-old only wakes up early for something she loves. And today these less-than-spectacular waves were skunking her.

She was about to call it quits on her search for some huge waves, when a familiar pickup truck, the Blanchards', pulled up beside Blue Crush. Her friend and teammate Alana was also on the hunt for some angry growlers.

A few months back, Bethany got second place at the National Scholastic Surfing Association (NSSA) Championships—Nationals, for short. Now, time was ticking, with only eight months to go until the next one. There, Bethany wanted to stand at the very top of the podium. First place was calling her name. She wanted gold.

Staring at the ocean, she bit her lip. These waves weren't going to help her get there. On an ideal surfing day in Kauai (pronounced Kah-oo-ah-ee), Hawaii, Bethany wouldn't have to wait long before, off in the distance, the sea would rise, higher and higher, until a bump formed. The bump would come flying toward her. That meant she'd have to move, and fast. Bethany couldn't be staring out to sea any longer; she needed to be facing the shore, ready to go. It was hard to paddle from a dead start, but Bethany would thrust both hands into the water, feeling the resistance, feeling her muscles work. Gently, the wave would catch her, lifting her up. But she wouldn't stop paddling, not yet. Soon, Bethany would feel the sudden pull of gravity. Belly still on her board, she'd tip over the wave. Then she'd push off the board with her hands, swinging her feet onto the board, fighting to keep her balance, and she'd stand. Going from one skill to the next, she'd move up, down, and through the wave, water spraying with each turn.

That was surfing.

Today, she scrunched her freckled nose. She wasn't sure, with these small waves, if she'd fully experience that sensation.

But now that Alana was here, being out in the water with her friend, even without killer waves, was better than sitting at her kitchen table for homeschooling. So as the sun rose, Bethany shouted goodbye to her mom and slipped into the warm water with Alana.

Lying on her red-white-and-blue surfboard in her red-white-and-blue bikini, Bethany stared out into the sea, waiting and waiting for that angry growler. So long, in fact, that her sun-bleached blonde hair was almost dry.

I hope the surf picks up soon, Bethany thought after thirty minutes of relaxing on her board. Alana, Alana's brother Byron, and their dad, Holt, were also hanging out on their boards, only fifteen feet away.

Back on land, beachgoers began to set up blankets and beach chairs. A few other surfers were preparing to join them in the lackluster waves.

Bethany drummed her fingers against the nose of her board while her left hand dangled in the water, a shiny blue watch on her wrist. She didn't know that a fourteen-foot tiger shark was also nearby, perhaps attracted to the reflection of Bethany's watch, which looked like the scales or eyeball of a fish.

Bethany knew there might be sharks in the water—tiger sharks live in tropical waters—but sharing the surf with sharks wasn't something that generally crossed her mind. Besides, sharks aren't easy to see. They don't swim the way they're shown in movies, with their black dorsal fin visible along the water's surface. Sharks swim beneath the surface, slow and quiet.

Had Bethany looked down and to her left, she might've seen the shark coming up through the crystal-clear water that day.

Instead, all Bethany saw was a gray blur as it broke the water's surface.

She felt her board lift and a few lightning-fast tugs, from jaws powerful enough to crack the shell of a 250-pound sea turtle.

But Bethany didn't scream.

She clung to her board and stayed on.

The shark let go and disappeared again beneath the surface.

Bethany noticed the red filling the water around her. It was startling. Was that blood? Was that . . . *her* blood?

Bethany stared at her own body in disbelief. She didn't feel any pain. And she realized her left arm, almost to her armpit, was gone.

A semicircle-shaped piece of her surfboard was gone too.

"I got attacked by a shark," she called out to Alana and the others. Shock, but also training, made her voice sound calm. Just two weeks ago, Bethany had taken a lifeguard emergency-response training class.

Don't panic. That was what Bethany had learned. And that was what she tried to do now.

In fact, Bethany was so composed that Alana thought she was joking about being bitten by a shark. No one had seen Bethany struggle; everything had happened so quickly, in less than three seconds. But then her friends saw the blood pooling in the water around her.

"Oh, my God!" Alana's dad cried.

Oh, my God was right.

"I can't believe this happened," Bethany said to no one in particular. Did *she* really lose an arm? Not feeling any pain, it was possible to imagine it had happened to someone else. But no. She blinked, and there was no denying she had only one arm.

Surfers used two. The front arm aimed where Bethany was going. The back arm balanced her. But now, *she only had one*, a thought that repeated in her head. Did a shark steal her dreams of becoming a professional surfer in a single bite?

How will I surf with one arm?

She couldn't. She didn't see how.

Bethany also had another thought, a funny one, considering the circumstances: *Will I lose my endorsements?*

One of Bethany's sponsors was Rip Curl. They'd sponsored her, giving her clothes, bikinis, and surfboards, since she was nine years old, after she won her first real surf competition.

But none of that mattered right now. All that mattered was saving her life.

To do that, Bethany first had to get out of the water. Unlike great white sharks, which commonly swim away after biting a human, tiger sharks are scavengers that have earned the nickname "man-eaters," along with "wastebaskets of the sea" because they'll eat anything they can find. Bethany had to reach the beach a quarter of a mile away, across a patch of reef, as quickly as possible.

Lying there, rocking on her board, her head also started to sway. She took a deep breath and blew out slowly. She wanted to give in to the dizziness and fear. Her body was screaming at her to panic, but she didn't see how that would help.

Already, with each second, Bethany was losing blood.

Thank God, she thought, trying to focus. *It's high tide*. That meant the water was higher and they could swim over the reef. Shallower waters would've meant having to go around the sharp coral and rocks.

From her training, Bethany knew time wasn't something she could waste.

Already, it would take fifteen minutes to reach the beach.

She looked to Alana, Holt, and Byron for help.

"Go!" Alana's dad yelled to Alana's brother. "Get to the beach! Call 9-1-1!"

Byron moved as fast as he could, paddling like a madman to get to dry land and call for help.

Holt pushed the back end of Bethany's board, sending her toward the reef. There, he was able to stand. She watched as he ripped off his rash guard, the stretchy shirt he wore to protect his skin, and wrapped it around what was left of her arm. He pulled it tighter and tighter. While he got her to the shore—while he got her help—his surf shirt would create a makeshift tourniquet to slow the bleeding to a trickle.

Get to the beach. Get to the beach, Bethany repeated silently to herself. Dizziness began to cloud her head. *Please, God, help me. God, let me get out of the water.*

With her right hand, Bethany seized the bottom of Holt's swim trunks, and he frantically pulled Bethany closer to the shores of Tunnels Beach.

CHAPTER 2

JUST HOLD ON

Bethany concentrated on staying calm, but as she glided over the reef toward the shoreline, doubt slipped into her mind. She could die from the shark attack. She saw it on Alana's face and the tears in her friend's eyes.

The air was warm, in the low 70s, but still, coolness seeped through Bethany's body, a sensation caused by loss of blood. Bethany's vision was spotty, her awareness of what was going on flashing in and out of focus.

But she heard voices. She was no longer in the water.

Holt shifted her from her ravaged surfboard to the warming sand, and those voices now hovered over her. She picked out Alana's and asked for water to quench an overwhelming sense of thirst. Alana dashed off, desperate to help her friend.

Someone took Holt's rash guard off Bethany's arm and replaced it with the leash from her surfboard, tying the new tourniquet tightly around what was left of her arm, a stump.

That stump was now beginning to hurt. Normally with minor injuries, pain is immediate, the body warning, *Watch out*. But with severe injuries, the body already knows it's in danger and first and foremost focuses on staying alive. The pain comes later.

"I want my mom," Bethany said weakly.

"Shh," someone said. "You'll be okay."

Another said, "You'll see your mom soon. Just hold on."

One by one, people covered her with brightly colored beach towels and kind words.

Bethany's head rolled to the side, staring at shins and knees, and she fought to stay awake. A Tupperware container dropped onto the sand beside her, a homemade first-aid kit. But no one was sure what to do or how to keep Bethany alive.

There was a rush of feet. "Everyone, please stand back," a man from a nearby home said. "I can help. I'm a paramedic."

It was almost as if the gathering of beachgoers and surfers exhaled all at once.

Alana was there too, a cup in her shaky hand. *Water, yes.*

"I know you're thirsty"—the paramedic checked Bethany's pulse—"but you're going to need surgery, and you need an empty stomach."

Surgery. The thought was fleeting, along with Bethany's glimpses of the worried faces hovering over her. She passed out.

Pain brought her back as the paramedic tugged on her makeshift tourniquet. She couldn't have been asleep long; she was still on the beach. Bethany bit her lip, both in an effort to keep from crying out and to stay conscious.

She felt a sudden wet coldness and jolted to see what caused it. A dog. One had wandered over and licked her, as if saying, "You're going to be okay."

Bethany wished her own dog, a shar-pei, was here. Snuggling with Ginger always made her feel better, and right now, that was what she needed. The paramedic's head and voice shook as he examined her wound and checked her pulse again. "She's lost a lot of blood."

Then why was she still lying on this sand? She needed to be at the hospital. Where was the ambulance? Hadn't Alana's brother called 911?

Help should be on its way. Help should've been there by now.

Alana's dad must've shared the same thought. He jumped to his feet, grabbed his board, and he and a few other surfers lifted Bethany onto it.

They raced through the trees toward the parking lot.

Bethany stared at the sun poking through the clouds and branches, her head bouncing with each hurried, jumbled step over and around the exposed tree roots.

The last thing she remembered was being slid onto the back of Holt's pickup truck, still on his surfboard. Yet when she opened her eyes, she was no longer in the pickup but instead on a stretcher in an ambulance.

Sirens blasted. Machines beeped. Needles pricked Bethany's skin.

Finally, she was on her way to the hospital.

Wilcox Memorial Hospital was on Kuhio (pronounced Koo-hee-oh) Highway, the same road the ambulance was currently on. The problem: It was a long road. Over thirty-five miles separated Bethany and the emergency room. And with Kuhio Highway being the only road to get around on, a traffic accident could block half the island from getting anywhere for a long, long time.

Through her cloudy mind, Bethany prayed there were no accidents that morning. The ambulance already moved slowly, winding around the narrow, tight turns of Hanalei (pronounced Han-ah-lay) Bay. She strained to imagine them passing each surf spot—the Bay, the Bowl, Pavilions, Pine Trees, Middles, Chicken Wings, Waikoko—until they rattled over a steel one-lane bridge. Bethany exhaled.

She knew that rumble, that feel of bouncing overtop the Hanalei River. The bridge meant they were leaving the North Shore beaches, and from there, the road straightened out. Now the ambulance driver could step harder on the gas pedal.

Bethany had about thirty more miles to go until she reached the hospital, and she needed to get there quickly.

Her hopes, her dreams, and her life all depended on it.

CHAPTER 3

COOL AS A CUCUMBER

Forty-five minutes had never felt so long. At last, the ambulance's sirens announced Bethany's arrival at Wilcox Memorial Hospital, where a medical team awaited them.

Bethany, blinking to stay awake, now knew she was where people could help her, and if she had made it this far, she was going to survive.

I'm going to make it, she assured herself again.

Moving through the halls of the hospital was a blur—a blur of voices and faces and lights and panic. None of the faces or voices was familiar. It was scary.

As she approached the X-ray room, Bethany wanted just one glimpse of her parents. Then she knew she'd feel better, and they'd know she was okay, that she was going to fight. Bethany twisted her head for a final look down the hallway before the doors of the X-ray room shut behind her, but she didn't see her mom or dad.

In the X-ray room, Bethany would've needed to be a doctor herself to understand everything going on around her. There were a lot of machines. The nurses took one X-ray after another. Some sort of fluid went through an intravenous (IV) line and into her good arm. Hospital people—nurses and technicians, Bethany guessed—endlessly poked and prodded her while various tests were run and more of her blood was drawn.

But the thing Bethany thought about most

was the thirst. She licked her dry lips, tried to swallow. Bethany was so thirsty she felt as if she'd been stranded in a desert for days.

A streak of blonde rushed into the room. Bethany exhaled, finally seeing her mom, followed by one of her brothers.

The three of them were a blubbering mess.

But after Dr. Rovinsky arrived, he assured them that Bethany had been as cool as a cucumber when the paramedics wheeled her into the hospital. "A lot of things had to have gone right for Bethany to make it to this point," her doctor said. He was referring to the high tide, to Holt's quick thinking to make a tourniquet, and to the fact that Bethany was, as he said, *cool as a cucumber*, keeping her heartbeat slow and pumping less blood. "She's got everything going for her."

Bethany's mom squeezed her hand.

The one hand Bethany still had.

Panic seized her again.

The feeling intensified as Dr. Rovinsky softly said, "You've lost your arm, Bethany. Now the focus is on saving your life."

Bethany only nodded, not quite trusting her voice to respond.

Then Dr. Rovinsky explained what would happen next. She'd be taken to an operating room, soundly asleep, unable to feel a thing. He'd try to save as much of the remaining portion of her arm as he could. The good news was the bite was clean, rather than a jagged tear. And she was young, her body in great physical shape to fight.

Everything her doctor said was meant to be comforting, but in that moment, Bethany could only think about how she wouldn't be able to surf with one arm.

How would she paddle out without the waves knocking her off her board?

If she got beyond the crashing waves, how would she paddle to catch a wave to surf?

Then how would she push herself from her belly to her feet?

The idea of getting to the point where she was standing on a board seemed impossible. But Bethany had a surge of hope. If she could get to her feet, she still had the more important arm. Meaning a surfer pointed where she wanted to go with her head and with her arm. Most surfers put their left foot toward the front of a board, but Bethany was what surfers called a "goofy foot" because she did it in reverse, with her right foot forward. This meant that Bethany used her right arm to lead, and it was her left arm that she'd lost to the shark bite. She could still point with her right hand, even if she didn't have her left hand trailing behind her for balance.

And she could learn to balance. She first learned to surf at the age of five. Only three years later, Bethany participated in her first real surf competition. She'd won, proudly returning home with a trophy and two new surfboards as her prize.

"Bethany?" her doctor said.

Bethany refocused on him.

Dr. Rovinsky had been telling her how he would thoroughly clean the wound because tiger sharks, as wastebaskets of the sea, have really dirty mouths and their bites have a high risk of infection.

"And we'll cut your nerves," he said, "which will cause them to retract and reduce the potential for phantom pain after the surgery."

Phantom pain?

Her doctor explained that sometimes people felt a mild to extreme pain in the area where a limb had been amputated. While the limb was no longer there, nerve endings could continue to send pain signals to the brain.

She nodded again, a bit overloaded with information and emotions, as Dr. Rovinsky squeezed her foot, then left.

Thank goodness for her goofball brother Timmy. He was clearly shaken up, but he could always make Bethany laugh. He could also get her water.

She remembered the paramedic's warning from the beach about needing an empty stomach for surgery, but she was too thirsty to care. More important, her brother didn't know about that rule.

Timmy brought her cup after cup of water, until it was time to head to the operating room.

There, a nurse asked her, "Do you want anything?"

Bethany licked her lips and swallowed. She was still thirsty, but now she was mostly tired. From the loss of blood, from a slew of tests, from being bitten by a fourteen-foot shark . . . she was exhausted. "Just to go to sleep."

The nurse smiled. "Okay, Bethany. Close your eyes and sleep."

CHAPTER 4

A NEW DREAM

Bethany puked, seconds after she woke up in the recovery room. Gross. She should've listened to the paramedic from the beach. Then maybe she would've saved herself from barfing water and cereal into a bedpan.

She blew out a long breath, feeling groggy and clearly sick to her stomach.

That was when Bethany saw her dad in a tiny hospital chair. She shifted in the bed, grinning, happy to finally see him. She hadn't seen him before her surgery because, ironically, *he* was about to have minor surgery on his knee. In fact, her surgeon kicked him out of the operating room so Bethany could stretch out on the table instead.

To greet her dad, she pressed her right hand against the bed to sit up straighter, but she had no way to push off on her left side.

Her dad's eyes fell on her arm. Or at least where her arm should've been. Now a wad of bandages stuck out three or four inches.

And that was it.

This was her new reality. It shouldn't have been surprising. Bethany knew the shark took her arm. But now, post-surgery, it felt more final.

Tears blurred her eyes. "I'm glad you're here, Dad."

He scooted his chair closer. "Bethany, I wouldn't be anywhere else in the world."

Bethany would be. She wouldn't be lying in a hospital bed with tubes hanging off her like she was an octopus. She'd be on top of a board, about to plunge over the crest of a wave. Or standing on the highest point of a podium, eagerly waiting to hold a first-place trophy. Wasn't that what she'd been working toward, another step closer to her future as a pro surfer?

Dr. Rovinsky gave a quick *tap-tap* on her door and strolled into the room in his blue scrubs. He also wore a big smile. It was comforting, along with his casual look: wavy brown hair and surfer tan. In fact, Dr. Rovinsky was a surfer himself, which made Bethany more confident about being in his care. They had something super important in common.

Or at least they used to.

Dr. Rovinsky spouted off details, as if saying them quickly would soften the blow.

She had undergone a traumatic amputation.

She'd lost 60 percent of her blood.

The wound was still open but covered by a bandage.

A second operation would happen in a few days to stitch her arm closed.

He'd check on her every morning.

"Listen," he said to Bethany's dad, sincerity in his voice, "the list of things Bethany will do differently will be long. But the list of what she'll be unable to do is short."

Did that second list include surfing competitively?

Sure, she'd had a moment of positivity before her surgery, when she realized she still had her arm she used to guide herself while navigating the waves. But how could she compete at the highest level, bringing in top scores during competitions, without her other arm balancing her out, essentially keeping Bethany on her board so she could perform tricks?

I can't be a professional surfer that way, she thought. *Not without both arms.*

Her surfing dreams were sunk.

Fear coursed through her. And when Bethany was freaked out, she ached for a way to feel more balanced so she wouldn't cry. Bethany reserved her tears for happy things.

Not having surfing in her life didn't make her happy.

She needed it, in any shape or form.

Think.

I won't wallow. I can adapt. I need to.

Then she realized: *Maybe I can still be close by the surfing action, as a photographer.*

Along with cooking and art, one of her hobbies was taking photos of flowers, and her brother Noah was a photographer. He could teach her. Yes, she decided. She didn't want to accept not being able to surf, but if she couldn't be the one deep in the barrel of a wave, she'd photograph people who could.

"Dad?" Bethany held back tears, fighting the ache in her belly that still made her want to think, *Woe is me*. "I want to be the best surf photographer in the world."

Her dad nodded and tried to smile. "I'm sure you will be."

CHAPTER 5

SEVEN DAYS WITHOUT SURFING MAKES ONE WEAK

Day one. After Bethany's surgery, she slept and slept. It was better that way, being unconscious. It gave her less time to think about what that shark had stolen from her. Also, she was legitimately tired. Sleep was all she wanted to do.

Day two. Bethany woke with a pain in her arm—her left arm. With her right hand, she felt for it, but there was only air. Bethany bit her bottom lip, chasing away the reminder that her limb was gone. The pain was phantom pain, the kind her doctor had told her could happen after an amputation.

Her chest rose, fell.

Bethany's dad walked in. Good. A distraction. Although Bethany didn't like how his eyes were bloodshot or how his brown hair seemed laced with added gray.

She put on a brave face, something she did repeatedly—for her parents, for her brothers, for every visitor who came to wish her well. For herself. "More reporters?" she asked.

Bethany's dad blew out a breath. "They're relentless." He moved aside a stuffed green frog and perched on the side of her hospital bed, careful not to disturb any tubes or wires. "But it's nothing for you to worry about."

She scrunched her nose, not liking that she made headlines. Bethany hadn't wanted to become a professional surfer in some ridiculous quest for fame. No, she surfed because she loved the sport, because everyone joked how salt water ran through her veins. What would they say about her now?

The idea of people pitying her left Bethany feeling itchy and uncomfortable.

"Are you up for another visitor?" her dad asked.

"Depends." Bethany gave him one of her sly smiles, where only half her mouth curled up.

"Alana."

Bethany nodded, eager to see her surf buddy. Alana, also a member of the Hanalei Bay girls' surf team, was part of her normal routine: Up early. On the water. Catching waves. Competing. Bethany needed something normal.

But what Alana saw didn't look normal to her. It showed on her face, and in how slowly she entered Bethany's hospital room.

Was it pity? Bethany hoped not.

Bethany's dad gave them privacy, but still, the

girls were silent—for one, two, three seconds—until Bethany said, "I'm still me."

She was, but Bethany also knew what Alana was thinking: *Even if you can't surf anymore?* Instead, Alana asked, "Are you okay?"

Bethany's smile was tight but sincere. The thought constantly running through her mind was *Why did this happen to me?* "I will be. I'm the same person on the inside."

Alana cautiously sat next to Bethany's bed and rubbed her eye. "I had a nightmare . . ."

Bethany only nodded. She'd had them too. Bethany had woken with her heart pounding, but her mom prayed with her, and Bethany was able to fall back asleep.

"I tried to surf," Alana continued. "I thought I saw a shark. But it was just a sea turtle."

"It'll take time," Bethany said, "for both of us."

Alana smiled at that, seeing Bethany more like the same positive girl she'd always been.

As others visited—Bethany's teammates and people from her church—they all realized that Bethany was simply *Bethany*.

It encouraged her, especially when Steve Cranston walked into her hospital room. He was from her sponsor Rip Curl and had flown in from another Hawaiian island, Oahu (pronounced Oh-ah-hoo).

Since the moment the shark took her arm, Bethany was worried that Rip Curl wouldn't want to work with her anymore and getting sponsored wasn't an easy thing. A few years ago when Bethany first started competing, her brothers were the ringleaders behind getting her a sponsor. Her brother Noah took photos of Bethany surfing and put together a website. Then he sent a slew of letters, introducing Bethany to the surfing world and all the big surf companies that make surfboards, clothing, and gear. Timmy also helped by filming Bethany surfing and made sure all those surf companies saw her in action.

It was a huge moment when Rip Curl said, "We want you!"

And now, Bethany was happy to see Steve had come all this way to visit her in the hospital, but she was also nervous about her future with Rip Curl.

Until he said, "Bethany, of course we still want to sponsor you."

In competitions? She had practically given up on that dream, resigned to only photographing pro surfers.

But here was Steve, saying they still wanted her. She nodded to herself. Maybe instead of giving up on her dream, she'd just have to fight harder to get to know her new body.

Day three. Bethany was on her feet! With the amount of time the nurses kept her in bed, you would think she had lost a leg, not an arm. So when the physical therapist had asked her if she wanted to take a walk, Bethany jumped at the chance, literally.

Except that being on her feet wasn't as freeing as she had hoped. The IV tubes, delivering her medicine, had to go with her. There she was, slogging down the hospital hallway, pushing a metal pole on wheels with a medicine bag swaying with each step she took. It was super awkward and a little uncomfortable. Mostly because everyone she passed gawked at the empty sleeve of her green polka-dot hospital gown.

They probably had seen the headlines and knew who she was.

That shark attack victim.

Bethany struggled with that idea. She didn't want to be known as *that shark attack victim* for the rest of her life.

Bethany breathed deeply and took another step. Then she put her left foot in front of her right foot again, and again. Bethany didn't want to see herself as a victim.

I'm a survivor.

This walk was a testament to that. Standing on her own two feet was inspiring. She let herself believe it again, that one day she'd stand on a Rip Curl surfboard during a major competition instead of watching from behind a camera's lens.

But first, there was *day four*, the day of her second surgery. Bethany didn't care too much for the details, but she understood the basics: The surgeon would take skin from under her armpit and pull it over her wound. Then he'd stitch her up.

"You'll be just fine," her dad said with a smile.

"I know," Bethany said. Although keeping her chin up was starting to wear on her, she still wanted to put on a brave face.

Bethany narrowed her eyes; her dad's current face wasn't so much *brave* as it was calculating.

"What is it?" she asked.

He scooped up her hand and swallowed. "Bethany, honey, two fishermen hunted down the shark."

Bethany felt a chill running through her. "How do they know that it's the one that . . ."

"The marks on your board match its mouth."

Those marks were sixteen inches wide. The shark was so large and heavy—around 1,400 pounds, more than ten times Bethany's weight—that an excavator was used to haul it from the water.

Bethany nodded. Her lungs were heavy. But then she smiled. "Now the beast can't hurt anyone else."

Day five. Yesterday's surgery made her groggy, and Bethany slept a lot. Every time Bethany woke, there were more nurses taking her temperature, fiddling with machines, and checking her tubes.

There were more balloons, stuffed animals, and flowers around her hospital room. A circus, safari, and garden all wrapped up in one.

There were also more uninvited visitors (aka

the press) trying to creep their way into Bethany's circus safari garden. Because of them, the hospital put security outside her door. That seemed silly to Bethany. When did she become someone who needed security outside her door? She was just the fun-loving, beach-bumming, small-town girl from Lihue (pronounced Lee-hoo-eh), Kauai.

It was time she reminded everyone of who she really was, herself included.

That meant pulling a mischievous gag on her nurses. She asked her brother to go home and get a fake rubber foot he often used to play practical jokes. The foot was pretty creepy; it looked *really* real.

Without anyone seeing, Bethany slipped the foot under her sheets. Then she waited.

Not long after—because the nurses visited like clockwork to check on her—one of them came into Bethany's hospital room.

"I think there's something wrong with my foot," Bethany groaned.

The nurse stopped dead in her tracks, confused. "Your foot?"

Bethany closed her eyes and moaned, feigning a lot of pain. "Yeah, I don't know what's wrong with it."

The nurse's eyebrows were furrowed with confusion as she pulled back the sheet and touched Bethany's so-called foot. When she yanked back her hand, her face was priceless, and a few shades whiter.

Bethany hooted with laughter, the nurse joining her after she realized it was all a prank.

Ah, that felt good, Bethany thought.

Day six. Bethany looked from her mom to her dad. "When can I get out of here?"

Bethany was tired of lying in bed. On a scale from one to ten, with a ten being "bored out of my mind," she was an eleven, going on a twelve.

She jumped up, grabbed a green balloon, and started bouncing it on her head.

One, two, three times.

Dr. Rovinsky walked into her room, and she forgot all about the fourth try. He checked her wound, something Bethany didn't dare to look at yet, then a big smile spread across his face. "How would you like to be released early?"

"Hooray!" Bethany shouted.

"But"—Dr. Rovinsky held up a hand as if to say, *Hold your horses*—"it's really important you don't get back in the water until after the stitches come out."

Yadda, yadda, yadda. All Bethany heard was: *back in the water.*

For six days, she'd been struggling with the idea of surfing again. Would she be able to get from her belly to her feet? If so, could she compete? And by compete, Bethany meant professionally.

But hearing her doctor so casually mention-ing her surfing again verified what Bethany felt deep in her bones: She would try. In fact, "Thanksgiving," Bethany declared. "I'm getting back in the water on Thanksgiving." The holiday was less than a month away.

CHAPTER 6

LIGHTS, CAMERA, ACTION

Before Bethany got back in the water, she'd have to get *out* of the hospital. Easier said than done.

All the media and press wanted to do was "sink their teeth" into Bethany, all eager to get the first interview from the girl who survived a shark attack.

She sat perched on the side of her hospital bed, surrounded by her family, ready to go home. Anxious to go home.

Two hospital security guards stepped away

from their posts at Bethany's door and into her room. "Ready?" one said.

Bethany nodded.

"Follow us," another said.

Things only got weirder from there, and Bethany felt like the main character in a spy film. Instead of going out the front entrance of the hospital—what any normal person would do—Bethany and her family snuck through a maze of hallways.

Then the security guards stopped at the back door of the hospital.

From there, the only place to go was outside.

But not home, as Bethany had hoped. Apparently, dozens of reporters were camped out on her front lawn, which was certainly not the best atmosphere for Bethany to rest and heal—something she needed to do if she wanted to be back in the water by Thanksgiving.

The guards heaved the door open. Light poured in. Though she couldn't go home, two police cars waited a few feet away, ready to take her to a family friend's house in Anahola Beach. Bethany fidgeted, not because of where she was going but because of how she'd be getting there. She was already the girl with one arm. She didn't want to be the girl with one arm in the back of a cop car.

Then she saw Blue Crush. The van's rust and chipped paint had never looked so good. She was thankful to be riding in style to her friend's house.

It was time for Bethany to heal. Not only for her body, but also for her soul. What better way for that to happen but for Bethany's dog to surprise her at her friend's house? All forty pounds of Ginger, with her many shar-pei wrinkles, wiggled with excitement at seeing Bethany. Bethany was more than happy to wrap her arm around her. For the first time since being bitten by the shark, Bethany cried. But they were happy tears.

* * *

The next day, a nurse came to change the dressing on her wound, and Bethany prepared herself. So far, she hadn't looked or so much as peeked at what was left of her arm.

She did now.

Oh my gosh, she thought.

The room spun, and she tried not to faint. It was a lot worse than she'd imagined.

I look like Frankenstein.

Long black stitches held her stump of an arm together.

Right then and there, Bethany knew she'd need help from someone much bigger than herself to get back in the water. Bethany needed to rely on her faith.

She took a deep breath and reminded herself that she would surf again, just as soon as those ugly stitches were out. And with the requests for interviews pouring in, it was clear everyone wanted to hear about Bethany returning to the water.

Oprah, *20/20*, *Inside Edition*, Ellen DeGeneres, Peter Jennings, *Life* magazine, *Sports Illustrated*, *The Early Show*, *Good Morning America*, *Today*, *CNN Live*, and a slew of others—they all wanted Bethany's story.

She wasn't eager to tell it.

That meant reliving the moment. That meant making herself uncomfortable by being in the spotlight.

Thankfully, her parents didn't push her.

About two weeks later, after the stitches came out and her arm looked less Frankenstein-y, Bethany rubbed her lips together, debating about the interviews. After some deliberation, she decided that she'd do it, she'd tell her story. The way Bethany looked at it, there could be other people facing a similar situation. Not similar in the sense that they were also bitten by a shark, but that they may be facing an obstacle that feels almost impossible, where they have to beat the odds, as she had.

Bethany believed she had survived because God had a plan for her. So she had one condition in agreeing to do any interviews: Bethany wanted to be open about her faith.

She started with an interview with *20/20*.

Like a small army, the production crew arrived in Hawaii and traipsed all around her hometown and beaches with their cameras. They were at it for hours and hours.

Chris Cuomo, the journalist who was going to interview her, also chatted with Dr. Rovinsky, her parents, the Hanalei Bay girls' surf team, some locals, and even Ralph Young, the man who caught the shark.

The whole process was surreal and felt a bit staged. Every shot was planned to get the best angle, the best light of the day, the best scenery. At one point, the crew filmed Bethany walking on the beach, her green dress flapping in the breeze. It was pretty awkward, knowing the cameras were on her, but she tried to look as natural as possible.

At her house, Chris followed her around her bedroom, which normally had stuff all over her floor, but not today. Today, her room was organized and she shared memories and pointed out some of her favorite things, such as a huge trophy she'd won during a competition. They even asked her to make a fruit smoothie, probably to show how she had adapted over the past few weeks to having only one arm.

So she whipped it up and felt proud about how she'd gotten pretty good at doing little things for herself. Bethany found ways to improvise, such as holding things—like the fruit while she chopped it—between her (clean) feet.

When it was time for the interview, Bethany wanted to keep it casual. Hair down. Shorts and a tee, showing off "Stumpy," the nickname she'd given her arm. And Bethany was barefoot. Indoors, that's how it's done in Hawaii. Rubber slippers, or flip-flops as non-Hawaiians call them, stay outside.

For the interview, lights, cameras, and microphones filled her living room. At the center of the room, Bethany and Chris sat facing each other in two wicker chairs.

The funny—and uncomfortable—thing was how the chairs were super close together. Their knees were almost touching, but Bethany guessed it was easier to get both of them in the same shot that way.

It was also funny that Chris, this big fancy reporter, had his sleeves rolled up, his legs crossed, and was also barefoot. That put Bethany more at ease, because the whole "being interviewed" thing was a little scary.

At least it wasn't live TV. For this interview, they'd record the whole thing and later edit out her more awkward moments when she blankly stared, not sure how to answer, or gave one-word replies.

When it was all said and done, after filming all day, the entire broadcast would be only ten minutes long, including all the footage they took of her island, her friends, and her family.

She could do this.

Just answer a few questions, she told herself.

Turned out, Chris had a ton of them, asking another question as soon as she answered one.

Where were you?

What were you doing?

How did it feel?

Were you scared?

How do you feel now? Sad? Angry? Shell-shocked?

Whoa.

Chris was only doing his job and he was nice about it, but the string of questions felt like an interrogation, and she fidgeted—a lot.

She did her best to make eye contact—something that was hard for Bethany when she was being put on the spot. To answer his last question about how she felt now, she said, "Well, I think that I should just have a positive attitude toward things and the challenges coming up and if I have a bad attitude, then it's not really going to make anything better."

Chris nodded, impressed with her strength. "During the attack, was there ever a moment where you started to panic?"

She pulled both feet onto her seat in a butterfly position, her knees pointed at the ceiling. "Not really. I think I figured out that if I panicked, then things wouldn't go as good as if I was calm. Like I was praying to God to help me and rescue me."

"Do you feel that for yourself you need to get back in the water, back onto the board?"

She gave one of her sly smiles. "Well, if I don't get back on that board, I'll be in a bad mood forever."

He laughed but then grew more serious. "Do you think you're going to surf again?"

Bethany shifted, one leg dangling over the side of the wicker chair. Her ankle moved in a circular motion. On the outside, she may've seemed uncomfortable, but it was being interviewed and not the question that made her feel that way. Bethany confidently looked Chris in the eye. "I think?" she said. "I *know* I'm going to surf again."

Competitively, she added in her head.

But she was getting ahead of herself.

One step at a time.

First, Bethany needed to see if she could paddle, stand up, and balance on a board. Then she'd take it from there. At the very least, she was excited to try. Lucky for her, Thanksgiving—the day she said she'd get back in the water—was only a few days away.

CHAPTER 7

IF AT FIRST YOU DON'T SUCCEED, TRY, TRY AGAIN

On the day before Thanksgiving, Bethany sat at her kitchen table, her schoolwork spread on the table in front of her. She had been homeschooled ever since the seventh grade. Before that, she'd gone to a normal elementary school. But once surfing picked up in her life, she had to be more flexible with her schedule, including school.

Right now, Bethany was anxious for surfing to pick up once again. She tapped her foot, feeling antsy. She knew Alana and her other surf buddies were at a secret surf spot in Kilauea (pronounced Kee-low-ey-ah), a small town on the northeastern shore.

She decided she'd go and watch.

But no, as soon as she had the thought, Bethany knew she wouldn't be able to simply sit on the sidelines. In fact, she couldn't make it one more day without being in the water and on a board. Bethany pushed aside her schoolwork, knowing she'd have to find time for her assignments later. "Mom?"

Her mom smirked, a smile so similar to her daughter's. "Let's go."

Bethany scurried to gather everything she'd need. Bathing suit. Board wax. A board.

A board. Bethany paused and instinctively touched Stumpy. Stumpy wasn't going to make this easy on her. Her balance would be off. She'd have only one arm to paddle with and, more of a challenge, only one arm to push herself up from her stomach to her feet.

Her eyes skimmed over a shortboard, a narrow type of board only five to seven feet long, which was what she usually used. Their size and shape make them ideal for quick turns and tricks because they cut through the water faster, which Bethany loved.

For now, though, she passed over her shortboard for a longboard. Longboards are eight to eleven feet long. They are also wider, making it easier to balance and paddle.

That was what Bethany needed today. It felt right. After all, longboards were the very first kind of surfboard, dating all the way back to the 1500s. And now Bethany would use a nine-foot longboard during her very first attempt at surfing with Stumpy.

She piled everything into the back of Blue Crush and resumed her foot tapping.

Thirteen-year-old Bethany competing in a surfing competition, less than three months before she was attacked by a fourteen-foot tiger shark.

On October 31, 2003, Bethany was attacked by a tiger shark at Tunnels Beach on the North Shore of Kauai, Hawaii. The beach gets its name from its many underwater caverns, which attract scuba divers and snorkelers.

Averaging 10 to 14 feet and 850 to 1,400 pounds, tiger sharks
are second only to great whites in number of attacks. The fish gets its
name because young tiger sharks have dark, vertical stripes.
With age, the markings fade and sometimes disappear.

AFTER LOSING HER
LEFT ARM IN THE
ATTACK, BETHANY HAD
A LOT OF SUPPORT,
FROM HER PARENTS
(PICTURED HERE),
TWO OLDER BROTHERS,
HER CHURCH,
HER COMMUNITY,
HER TEAMMATES,
HER COACH, AND,
OF COURSE, ALL HER
FANS. SHE RECEIVED
HUNDREDS OF LETTERS
EACH WEEK!

During her recovery and training, Bethany had to relearn how to surf with
her new body. A handle on her board helped, which Bethany used to remain
on her board while "duck diving" beneath a crashing wave.

Less than eight months after the shark attack, Bethany was at Trestles Beach in California, readying herself for the 2004 National Scholastic Surfing Association (NSSA) Championships.

In 2004 at the Teen Choice Awards, Janet Jackson presented Bethany with the Courage Award, the first time the honor was ever awarded.

BETHANY TOLD HER STORY IN HER 2004 MEMOIR, *SOUL SURFER: A TRUE STORY OF FAITH, FAMILY, AND FIGHTING TO GET BACK ON THE BOARD.* HERE SHE IS AUTOGRAPHING A COPY.

At the 2005 National Scholastic Surfing Association (NSSA) Championships, Bethany shredded the waves and finally achieved her goal. She won first in her division!

BETHANY'S STORY WAS ALSO TOLD IN THE FILM *SOUL SURFER*, STARRING ANNASOPHIA ROBB AS BETHANY, THOUGH BETHANY PERFORMED HER OWN SURF STUNTS! SHE ATTENDED THE PREMIERE IN NEW YORK CITY AND POSED FOR PICTURES.

In 2007, Bethany finally achieved her ultimate goal of becoming a professional surfer and began traveling around the world for competitions and trainings. By the end of 2008, she was ranked #14 in the world.

In 2013, Bethany married Adam Dirks. The next year, they competed in the television competition show *The Amazing Race*, where Bethany was the first contestant to compete with an amputated arm. Their hand gestures are called the "shaka," which is a sign of friendship among the various ethnic cultures that live in Hawaii.

Look at that wave! In Pe'ahi, Maui, the waves grow infamously big (sometimes up to fifty feet!), earning the nickname of "Jaws." In 2016, Bethany surfed there and caught her largest wave ever. Plus, she did it only six months after giving birth to her first child.

When Bethany was inducted into the Surfers' Hall of Fame in 2017, she wrote the message *Always Hope*. Her message, along with her footprints and right handprint, are now cemented into a walkway in Huntington Beach, California. Her prints lie in front of a statue of the great Duke Kahanamoku, who popularized the sport of surfing.

Her whole family was with her. Even her dad took off work waiting tables at the Princeville Hotel to be there. "Bethany," he said, "I'm sure you can do whatever you put your mind to."

Boy, did she need that pep talk. It was easy to lie in a hospital bed or sit in front of a camera and proclaim she'd surf again. Those were just words. Now she had to act. Bethany had to *actually* surf, and she felt she had a lot riding on it. Failing at one of the most important things to her was beyond terrifying. But she also needed this day to go well to give her hope for the future, that maybe, just maybe, she'd be able to surf competitively again.

No pressure or anything.

Her mom pulled Blue Crush off the road to park, and Bethany navigated a small trail until her feet hit the sand. There, she stopped, excitement and nerves pumping through her body.

Sandbars had formed throughout the water.

That was a good thing. The sand affects how a wave is going to break, and *this spot*, Bethany thought, *is about as good as it ever gets.*

Her surfing buddies picked a good one today. Her eyes danced from girl to girl—Kristen, Camille, Jackie, some in the water and some on the beach—and then onto Alana.

"Bethany!" Alana called, and ran to Bethany. "You're here!"

Yes, she was.

And, thankfully, their little secret spot meant that the press was not. There wouldn't be headlines splashed everywhere about Bethany attempting her first surf after the attack.

She stretched, watching the water to learn the patterns of the waves. It was a special kind of skill, and Bethany was good at "reading" the ocean.

She inhaled the familiar salty air. "You can do this," Bethany said aloud.

"You can," Alana echoed.

Her brother Noah held up his video camera. "And I'll capture every second of it."

Bethany laughed, not sure if that was a good or bad thing.

The afternoon sun warmed her face. The water called to her.

It was go time.

Side by side, Bethany and Alana walked into the water, just as they did on the day of the shark attack. Bethany wanted to pause, to savor the moment, but she was too eager to go deeper into the surf.

She dropped to her stomach and plunged her right arm into the white water, all churned up from the crashing waves. Instinctively, she gave Stumpy a turn to stroke, and sucked in a breath when nothing happened. Stumpy couldn't paddle.

Forget it, you're going to fail, she thought.

"Go, girl!" her dad called, swimming beside her.

Water splashed onto her face and soaked through the bandage on Stumpy. She tasted salt water on her lips and a feeling washed over her that she was home after a month-long trip away.

Bethany thrust her right hand into the soupy water again, and again.

It was hard, like doing a one-arm push-up.

But she was paddling, slowly. Yes, she could do this. But she still doubted if she'd be able to pop up from her belly to her feet with one arm. She didn't want to fail.

Farther out, waves crashed. Big, unbroken blue waves. Alana paddled through the soup and toward them. Her goal was to get beyond the waves so she could surf one in. She gripped her board with both hands and shoved down, diving underneath a wave. Alana emerged on her board, from her "duck dive," in the calmer water.

Bethany slowed, her arm burning. Her pulse raced with nerves, not sure how she'd dive—and stay on her board—as Alana had. Bethany decided that'd be a problem for another day. Today, she'd surf the smaller ankle slappers.

She'd be a "grom" again, a new surfer learning how to stand on a board in the rolling, white water.

And that was okay.

One step at a time, she reminded herself.

Bethany got in position, waiting for a smaller wave. She let a few pass, rocking on top of her board, getting used to being back on the water and doing what she worried she'd lost forever.

She felt a wave pick her up, and her gut screamed, *Go!*

Normally, she'd hold on to both sides of the board and pop up to her feet. That wouldn't work anymore. With her right hand, she fanned out her fingers—and pushed!

Off balance, Bethany immediately tumbled to the side and went under. The surfboard's cord tugged on her left foot, caught in the wave she missed.

When she broke the surface, she sucked in air and slapped the water, frustrated.

But she knew she'd try again. And again.

Still, she couldn't get up to her feet. Fear coursed through her. Standing was just the first step to getting her dreams back on track, and she was struggling to do even that.

"Bethany," her dad shouted. "Try it one more time. This one will be it!"

She blinked water from her eyes and looked at her dad. She saw confidence there. "Do you want help?" he asked. He could push Bethany and her board onto the wave.

Bethany shook her head. "I have to do this on my own."

"Okay," he said. "It may help to put your hand on the very center of your board."

She licked her lips. That made sense. She'd have better balance. Back in position, she surveyed the water. A tiny wave rolled through. Bethany caught it. She planted her hand—up by the nose, smack-dab in the center of her board—and swept one foot, and then the other, onto her board. A look of awe crossed her face as her fingertips left the board. She wavered, bending as if to touch the board again for balance. But Bethany didn't need it. She straightened, riding the wave in.

And just like that, she had done it.

Who cared if it was a junk wave? Not Bethany. Her friends and family didn't care either. Their cheers filled the beach.

Bethany thought of surfing as an addiction, a rush indescribable to anyone who hadn't experienced it. And when it grabbed you, it never let go.

Even after a shark attack.

That afternoon, Bethany didn't think about the shark. Not once. She was too focused on recapturing her dreams.

CHAPTER 8

TIME TO MAKE SOME NOISE

It was after Bethany's first time surfing again that the idea of sharks being in the water sank in. While it was never in the back of her mind before, surfing with sharks was something that made her very afraid now. But she'd fight that fear. She'd keep getting in the water. She'd focus on the waves and how stoked she was to be surfing again. She'd keep her sights set on her dreams. If she ever felt uneasy, she'd take a break and get out of the water. And that was okay.

Bethany was determined to train. Every day. Twice a day. Some days, up to seven hours.

Each morning began much the same way: Bethany's mom clicked on the television and put on the local island weather channel. Next step: Her mom needed coffee. While she brewed a strong cup for herself, she listened to the forecast and also the buoy reports. Those were really important and helped Bethany's mom pick the best spot for her daughter to surf that day.

"Cloudy, but no rain this morning, Bethany," her mom hollered one morning. In the past, surfing in the rain wasn't a bad thing, which is good since it rains almost daily in Hawaii, if only for a short burst. But after her run-in with the shark, it was hard not to think how the rain would make the water murky, and how that murky water could be hiding the jaws of a shark or could cause the beast to mistake her for food.

But shark attacks aren't that common, and

part of Bethany thought that it simply couldn't happen to her again. Sharks just didn't come around enough.

Once is weird; twice won't happen, she often told herself.

It was good to put the actual frequency of shark attacks into perspective. It was even better to put the number of shark attacks into perspective by combining them with funny facts:

Each year, air fresheners injured two hundred times more Americans than sharks did.

Buckets and pails injured eight hundred times more Americans than sharks did.

And toilets injured three thousand times more Americans than sharks did.

Regardless of the silliness and the relatively low number of shark attacks, Bethany was someone who was now part of those stats, and she sighed, relieved that rain wasn't in the forecast, so there'd be non-murky water awaiting her. She didn't need her mind playing tricks on her, imagining things that weren't there.

From her bed, Bethany called to her mom, "How's the wind?"

While still tucked under her covers, Bethany started each day with a devotional, which is a fancy way of saying she spent time with God, praying and reading her Bible. That day's Bible verse was about how God had a plan for everyone. Bethany believed it to be true. It was why she thought she was bitten by that beast and thrust into the limelight—so that she could inspire others and share her faith. And she'd very happily keep surfing as part of God's plan for her.

Bethany added, "Are they offshore winds?"

"For now!" her mom responded from the kitchen.

Bethany smiled. She liked those. Onshore winds—the kind that blew from the ocean toward land—often caused choppy water. In other words, not great surfing conditions, especially with Stumpy affecting her balance. But good offshore winds—ones that blew from land out to sea—delayed the breaking of a wave. This made it steeper and more powerful.

But would she be able to balance in these conditions? In more ways than one, Stumpy was an adjustment.

So, Bethany often thought, *I'll adjust*.

If she wanted to be a pro surfer, there was no other way around it. During competition, for the judges to give her a score for how well she rode the wave, Bethany had to be completely on her feet, her hand no longer on the board.

That took a lot of balance, and she needed her whole body to be strong.

To help, over the past few weeks she'd been using resistance bands and swimming laps. Yes, with one arm. She ran on the beach, which helped to strengthen her lungs, allowing her to hold her breath longer underwater. She lifted weights. And did stomach crunches. That last one helped tone her core muscles, the ones she needed while twisting and turning on her surfboard.

On dry land, Bethany had also spent a lot of time on—and falling off—a balance board and a skateboard. In the water, she spent a lot of time on—and falling off—her longboard and, eventually, a six-foot shortboard.

Being back on her normal shortboard was a big achievement, and she had the bumps, bruises, reef rash, and coral scratches to prove it.

Not like she'd stop. Not with how much she loved being back on her shortboard or with how Nationals kept creeping closer and closer.

Which is exactly why she needed to train.

Today, with no rain and favorable winds, the surfing conditions sounded promising. But there were still more factors to consider: wave height and wave length. "What kind of waves do we have?" she called from bed to her mom.

"Got some big, tall ones, coming in every eighteen seconds."

That also made Bethany smile. Waves came in sets, a few waves per set. And surfers wanted the time between each wave to be nice and long. To put it simply, the longer the period between each wave, the more power the wave would have when it broke. And Bethany wanted powerful waves to practice on.

Luckily, that day's buoy report was telling Bethany she was probably in for some gnarly waves. God was giving her a good weather day out on the water. As she put aside her Bible and got out of bed to get ready, she was nervous, yet stoked. Up until today, Bethany had spent a lot of time surfing on smaller waves, just standing up and figuring out how to catch them. Each time, she felt better and better about her surfing abilities. But she couldn't stay on the small waves forever. Pro surfers didn't surf those types of waves.

Bethany said a quick prayer for safety—and

no sharks—and came out from her bedroom. "Tie me?"

Her mom double knotted the back of Bethany's bikini top and pulled her hair into a ponytail. "Ready?"

Bethany grinned, even as a sharp pain radiated through her arm—her missing arm. Stumpy still caused her phantom pain. "I'm ready." She and her mom jumped in Blue Crush.

With the next national competition only months away, Bethany wanted to move on from the ankle slappers to the bigger waves. That required getting past the crashing waves to the calmer water. There, she'd lie on her belly, next to the other competitors, and wait for an approaching wave to catch.

During each round at Nationals, the judges would be looking for a variety of difficult maneuvers, connected to other skills, with a powerful speed and flow.

Bethany knew a move called a backside snap

often caught the eye of judges. First, she'd ride down the wave. Toward the bottom third of the wave, she'd twist on her board so that she was no longer riding *down* the wave but *up* against it. Then, once she felt the board connecting with the top of the breaking wave, she'd snap. If done correctly, a snap would look like a U-turn. The skill was quick and powerful with a flashy spray of water flying up into the air.

That was what she'd want. That was what the judges would want to see when they determined what score out of ten to give her.

Then, as soon as her backside snap was complete, Bethany would study the wave, trying to figure out what skill the wave wanted her to do next.

Of course, to really impress the judges, Bethany wanted to get tubed in a barrel ride. For that skill, she'd surf through a hollow wave before it crashed. When she popped out of the other side, the spectators and judges always went nuts. It was a feeling she lived for, but barrels were hard to spot and even harder to get perfect. What was that old saying? Practice makes perfect.

Bethany believed it.

When they reached the surf spot, she was eager to get into the water to do just that: practice. And this time, she'd ride the big, blue waves. She ran toward the water, eyeing the waves, the sand shifting from loose to harder packed the closer she came. The conditions were good ones, just as her mom had predicted. Bethany landed belly first on her shortboard and paddled through the white water of a wave that had already crashed. Her muscles ached, but in a good way. As a big wave was about to crash, she tried to push down on the nose of her board, so she could ride underneath the breaking wave.

Her arm slipped on her board.

The wave pummeled her, tossing and turning her under the water, giving Bethany a dirty licking.

She emerged from the water, coughing. Frustrated. Instead of being beyond the wave, in the calmer water, the wave had taken her like a rag doll toward the shoreline.

She tried again. Each time, with only one hand, Bethany found it hard to push down on her board hard enough to submerge it under the water. The times she managed to duck dive, she struggled to stay on her board under the wave. If she managed that, her next challenge was controlling her board back to the surface once the wave passed.

Most of the time, she wiped out. She got mouthfuls of salt water. She got stuck in the impact zone, where the waves broke. Again and again.

It was defeating. Maddening, really. She'd never be able to perform the maneuvers and skills the judges were looking for if she was unable to reach the big waves.

Later, her eyes burned with the promise of tears as she told her dad. It didn't take him long before he had a genius idea.

"See here?" he said. Her dad had attached a handle to the nose of her shortboard. It would allow her to push, hold on to, and control the board.

He said, "Grab on to this."

Bethany's eyes lit up. "Now I can dive under the wave."

He nodded. "Now you can get past the big ones."

Her dad was good like that, helping her in any way he could to succeed. Both her parents were. Her mom and dad had spent years surfing themselves, happily putting Bethany on a board at the age of five. Surfing was like learning to ride a bike because it took time and a lot of hard work. By the time Bethany was seven years old, she could catch waves without her parents' help. But she still needed a professional coach, especially now as she was adapting to her new body—and now that she could finally get beyond the big waves again.

Bethany had a great coach with great ideas. The days and weeks went on. Even on the days when the conditions weren't stellar, they trained. The way her coach saw it, the waves could be gnarly at Nationals or they could be weak. She had to be ready for anything.

Problem was, Bethany was having trouble paddling fast enough to catch her practice waves. Only having one arm made it a challenge to create enough power to propel herself faster and faster.

During a competition, this would be a major obstacle because only one surfer was able to ride a wave at a time. If Bethany wanted the wave to be hers, she needed to get to it first.

On the beach, she stood next to her coach, droplets rolling off her nose while she listened to his advice before she got back in the water.

"Kick your feet," he suggested. "It'll help you go faster."

At 5 foot 7 inches tall, Bethany's feet extended past her shortboard. It was worth a try. But she still had trouble picking up speed.

"Grunt," he said.

She shielded her eyes from the sun to see him better. "What?"

"Grunt. Don't be afraid to make some noise out there!"

No way, she thought. That was embarrassing.

"Just try it."

What did she have to lose? So she did. Bethany made some noise.

And her coach was right.

She propelled herself faster, and the next time, Bethany grunted even louder.

Bethany caught the wave!

It put a big smile on her face. So far, she'd gone from her longboard to a shortboard. She'd gone from the small waves to the big waves. Now she had to go from grom skills to more impressive skills. Except, she told her coach, "I'm having a really hard time without two arms on the big waves."

"So," her coach said, "imagine you have two."

It was worth a try. At night when she dreamed, Bethany still had both arms. On her next few waves, she took his suggestion, picturing two arms, and she started to feel more comfortable on a board again.

Bethany trained and trained. She had good days. Days when she felt confident. And days when she mumbled with frustration to herself, "Come on, Bethany."

On her last ride, she had glided out onto the shoulder—or the least steep part—of the wave. She had wanted to stay in the wave's pit, where the wave was the steepest. She tried to do a roundhouse cutback, where she'd make a figure eight to ride back into the breaking wave, but she messed up the skill. Bethany had to bail.

Her coach watched from the beach.

Bethany exhaled sharply and refocused. On her next wave, she dropped into it and glided deep into the trough—the lowest part of the wave—where Bethany whipped a bottom turn. She was out in the open face of the wave, riding in front of the break. There, she put on a show, carving from turn to turn.

As the wave petered out, Bethany smiled.

Her coach was smiling too.

She caught her breath, and paddled back out to do it all over again.

The next time, she stayed on the lip—or the uppermost part of the breaking wave—and surfed off the top of the wave. In the air, she crouched low and used her right hand to grab the board, known as a mute grab. Bethany and her board landed together on the water's surface again.

She'd done it. A mute grab wasn't an easy skill. But was Bethany ready for Nationals?

She sure hoped so.

For the past seven months, she'd trained harder than ever before. Her hand and feet were constantly wrinkled like prunes from being in the water so often.

Bethany was living proof that where there was a will, there was a way. She would do everything she could to ensure she'd deliver at Nationals.

CHAPTER 9

GOING FOR GOLD

Sitting on the rocky beach, Bethany rubbed wax over her shortboard. She didn't want her feet to slip when she was competing. Nerves fluttered around her belly like butterflies, their wings haphazard and quick.

Eight months had flown by since the shark attack, and now Bethany was in California, awaiting the start of the NSSA Championships.

Over the next few days of the competition, she had six rounds of surfing in front of her. Hopefully. Each round would be twenty to thirty-five minutes long, when Bethany would try to catch as many waves as possible. It wasn't about quantity, though. It was about quality: Catching *great* waves was her goal.

But that was what the other girls in her heat were thinking too. The judges counted only the top two scores of each girl.

Only some of her competitors would advance past the initial three rounds of preliminaries. Then fewer and fewer would survive the quarter-finals and the semifinals and eventually run into the crashing waves with a board under their arm for the final heat.

Bethany badly wanted to surf all six rounds.

And it seemed as if more than just the judges wanted to see how Bethany would perform in her first contest after the attack. The media, the spectators, the other competitors, her fans, her family—they all did.

No one looked at her in a mean way, but as the competition progressed, everyone was curious and all eyes were on Bethany. Everyone watched as she carried her waxed board out toward her first waves of the competition. Everyone wondered: Would Bethany score well enough in the preliminaries to go on?

The answer?

Yes.

Would her scores during the quarterfinals allow her to advance?

Yes.

Could Bethany—with one arm—survive the semifinals and line up for the final heat?

Yes, she could.

And suddenly that heat was only a few minutes away.

Bethany had made it to the final round at Nationals. One arm or two arms, she would've put in the work regardless, but one less limb hadn't held her back from getting there.

That was an accomplishment in and of itself, and one that made Bethany feel proud.

But she wasn't done. Last year she got second place. This year she wanted to be the best, and there was only one more round to go: the round that would determine the competition's champion.

Sitting beside her parents on Lower Trestles Beach, she licked her lips and watched the waves. Reading them.

It had been six hours since the semifinals. Bethany's muscles still burned, she still tasted the dried salt water on her lips, but her leg bobbed in anticipation of getting back in the water.

"How are you feeling, Bethany?" her mom asked.

The sky was clear, the temperature in the 70s. Wind was coming from the west. That meant onshore winds—the kind of breeze that sometimes made the waves not so good—but Bethany still saw waves she could work with. She told her parents, "I'm feeling good."

"I see some waves breaking in a line," her dad said, echoing Bethany's thoughts.

She nodded. It was a good thing when her eye

could follow a wave as it broke from left to right, or right to left. Waves that broke all at once were harder to ride, sometimes unsurfable. It was known as a closeout.

Her dad squeezed Stumpy to show his support, the stub now simply a part of Bethany. "Know where you want to line up?"

She did. She saw where the waves were starting to break. With her eyes, she created an imaginary line from the water to a blue tent on the rocky beach.

"There," she said, pointing.

When she was out in the water, she'd find that tent and line up with it. That was where she needed to be in order to take off on a wave.

Then she'd need to surf at least two great waves to get two great scores. It may sound simple to put a combination of skills together and score well, but it can be very challenging.

In past contests, sometimes nature won and the wave took control. Before Bethany knew it, the wave would drag her to the bottom of the ocean, giving her a dirty licking. Those times, she got no score at all—and some bruises. Not to mention her bruised pride.

Bethany didn't want that to happen today.

Her mom grabbed her hand.

It was time to pray, something they did before every heat. First, Bethany prayed for the safety of everyone. Then she prayed for wisdom to help her pick the best waves. She also gave a quick plea to be at the right place at the right time to help her catch those good waves. Even with all her hard work, it'd be difficult to paddle faster than her competitor if they were both going for the same wave.

The air around her vibrated, laced with excitement.

The other five girls in the final round, with their boards tucked under an arm, navigated the stone-covered beach to the water's edge.

Bethany stood to join them. She passed the five judges, all lined up in a row behind a table.

She passed the many spectators lounging on chairs and beneath umbrellas. She passed a row of photographers, some down on one knee for the perfect angle. And she wished the other girls good luck.

Her heart pounded in her chest.

She felt the eyes on her.

The waves splashed around her ankles before receding.

The horn blasted.

The competition began.

Bethany took off running toward the blue California water.

All that mattered right now was the next thirty-five minutes, the length of this final round.

On her belly, she paddled. Water splashed into her face and eyes. She shook her head and kept going through the white water. Up ahead, a wave was beginning to crash. Bethany squeezed the trusty handle on her board, used her body weight to push down, and duck dived beneath the breaking wave.

Bethany emerged and instantly plunged her arm into the water again to paddle. Once she was beyond the waves where the water was calm, she looked to the beach. There was the blue tent. She aligned herself with it. Bethany was lined up.

Her competitors were scattered about. Some close. Some farther away. All of them were hoping they were in the right spot to catch a perfect 10 wave. They all waited.

One of the girls, Carissa, made the first move. Like a runaway train, she started paddling. Other girls did too. Bethany knew she wouldn't be able to catch up with a competitor as fast as Carissa when she had a head start, and sure enough, Carissa reached the wave first. All that the other girls could do was watch as Carissa rode the wave and set the pace for the final heat with a score of 7 out of 10. Another girl answered back on the next wave, the judges announcing a score of 7.50.

With only one surfer at a time able to ride a wave, Bethany was forced to wait. Then, off in the distance, she saw a slight ripple of a wave forming. She was first to make her move. She paddled, she grunted, she kicked. The other girls raced behind and beside her. Bethany gave it everything she had and became the closest. It was her wave to surf.

Hers.

Thanks to all her practice, she popped up to her feet. With a huge smile on her face, she carved across the wave, turning and cutting, until it was time to kick out of the wave. She sank into the water, with an even bigger smile on her face.

Bethany lived for this. Surfing was like breathing, something that was a necessary part of her existence.

And in her very first contest since coming face-to-face with a tiger shark, she wasn't merely surfing. She was competing.

Bethany was a competitor.

But so were the other girls.

They were catching waves. Good waves. They were performing great maneuvers. Time was ticking away.

But Bethany wasn't done yet. She had a sixth sense when it came to the ocean. She saw another wave forming in the distance, and her stomach fluttered. She knew it was going to be what's known as a set wave.

A bomb.

The biggest wave to come through.

And Bethany was the only one in the position to catch it—if she paddled her butt off.

With her arm throbbing, she reached the wave. Barely. She held her breath; it was going to be a late drop onto the wave. That meant getting to her feet faster than ever.

She did, glancing quickly at her board to make sure her feet were in the right spots. Bethany shifted her weight back and made the drop.

Now it was go time.

Bethany did a bottom turn, propelling herself back onto the top of the wave. There, she tore it up, doing one rapid turn off the top of the wave—called a lip slash—after another. Each time, she threw up loads of spray.

The beach erupted with noise.

In that moment, Bethany proved she was back.

She'd always be a contender.

Bethany would be a professional surfer, just as she had always dreamed. One arm or two arms, it didn't matter. She was born to do this.

The horn blasted again, signaling the end of the final heat of Nationals.

CHAPTER 10

ALWAYS FEARLESS

Nationals were over. But did Bethany win?

Not this time.

Carissa was the best that day.

Bethany came in fifth.

Naturally, she was upset. But it was okay. When she first set her goal of standing at the top of the podium, she had two arms. With only one, no one had expected her to surf again. But Bethany and Stumpy had. She'd done her best and became one of only six girls who surfed all six rounds at Nationals.

She also remembered her dad's words from the first time she surfed after the attack. "Bethany," he had said, "I'm sure you can do whatever you put your mind to."

So Bethany would keep training. She still had her mind set on winning Nationals.

And the next year, fifteen-year-old Bethany was the best that day in the under-eighteen surf championships. She did it. She won, beating second place by nearly four points.

Maybe it took longer than she wanted, but Bethany fearlessly earned the title *champion*.

And that other goal she had for herself—becoming a professional surfer? Bethany achieved that two years later.

But Bethany didn't stop there. The thing with dreams is that they can come in many forms, and as Bethany grew, her dreams grew with her. At one time, Bethany was *that shark attack victim*, but she didn't stay a victim for long. Bethany has proven she's much more than that.

Role model

After Bethany's shark attack, she didn't feel like a role model, but others certainly saw her that way. During the 2004 Teen Choice Awards, fourteen-year-old Bethany took the stage to accept a special Courage Award in front of an energetic crowd.

Bethany has also put her good heart to work helping and inspiring others. At fifteen, she traveled to Thailand after the country was ravaged by a tsunami, where earthquakes under the sea caused a one-hundred-foot wave to hit the shoreline. There, she participated in a surfing exhibition and shared her story of how she overcame tragedy, along with encouraging kids to face their fears and get back in the water, as Bethany had done when she was thirteen.

TV and film star

Along with television interviews, Bethany spent some time in front of the camera in other ways. At seventeen years old, she put on her producer hat as she told her story in the documentary *Heart of a Soul Surfer*. Of course, a documentary about Bethany had to star Bethany, and so did a handful of other films and television programs. Thirteen-year-old Bethany played herself in various television series, such as *Switched!*, then, at twenty-four years old, in films like *Dolphin Tale 2*. She was also a contestant, at age twenty-four, on the reality television competition show *The Amazing Race*. In the 2011 film *Soul Surfer*, starring AnnaSophia Robb as Bethany, Bethany herself hit the waves to perform the surf stunts. Bethany's latest film appearance was in the 2018 documentary *Unstoppable*.

Author

Another way Bethany has told her story is through books, beginning with her bestselling autobiography, *Soul Surfer*. She's also written numerous spiritual devotional books, as well as books about living a healthy life, and a book in which she answers questions from her fans.

Mother and wife

At twenty-three years old, Bethany put on a white dress, clipped a white veil and white flowers in her hair, and said, "I do," to Adam Dirks, a youth minister. Less than two years later, Bethany and Adam welcomed their first child, Tobias, whom Bethany has called her surfing baby. Bethany and Adam welcomed their second child, Wesley, in 2018.

Athlete

At twenty-four years old, Bethany earned the title Favorite Comeback Athlete by the Nickelodeon Kids' Choice Awards after winning multiple surfing competitions, such as the O'Neill Island Girl Junior Pro tournament and the Surf n Sea Pipeline Women's Pro. It's an accomplishment for any surfer to be ranked in the top twenty in the world, and Bethany held a spot in the top twenty for a few years—without being given any slack from her fellow competitors or the judges. If anyone were to offer Bethany favors, she'd politely refuse them. She wanted to compete fairly, and has, all over the world, in places including Australia, Nicaragua, Indonesia, Western Samoa, France, Portugal, Spain, Thailand, England, Japan, Mexico, Fiji, Tahiti, Peru, the Maldives, Brazil, and more.

All of Bethany's hard work and dedication to surfing paid off. At twenty-seven years old, Bethany was inducted into the Surfers' Hall of Fame. As part of the honor, on the cement in front of the Duke statue at Huntington Beach, California, Bethany left impressions of her feet and right hand, and wrote the message to *Always Hope*.

While surfing is Bethany's passion, she's also taken to a board in different ways. For example, she's added professional wake surfer to her résumé, riding the currents behind a boat as a wake boarder.

And at twenty-five, Bethany got behind a boat in a whole new way. Well, technically behind a Jet Ski. With waves over thirty feet high, it's hard for any athlete to paddle fast enough to catch them. So when Bethany had her eye on a fifty-foot wave known as Jaws, she had the help of a Jet Ski to get into position to catch the wave. Already standing on her board, she held on to a cord and was towed behind the Jet Ski. When in position, she let go and surfed a wave so big it took her nearly thirty seconds to ride it.

Afterward, Bethany proclaimed, "I just got the heaviest, biggest wave of my life!"

So far.

COMMON SURF TERMS AND MANEUVERS

aerial: riding the board into the air and landing back on the wave

barrel: the tube, or the curl of the wave

bomb: an exceptionally large wave, in comparison to other waves

bottom turn: the first turn at the bottom of a breaking wave

carve: to surf with numerous turns and cutbacks

chop: bumpy ocean and wave conditions that are rough due to strong winds and/or currents

closeout: when a wave breaks all at once, with no shape or shoulder

crest: the top and highest point of a wave

cutback: a turn cutting back toward the breaking part of the wave

drop: the moment after paddling in and standing up to ride a wave

duck diving: the technique of pushing the surfboard under and through a breaking wave

fade: pointing toward the breaking part of the wave, then turning sharply in the direction the wave is breaking

flat: with no waves, or with no surf

floater: surfing on the top of the breaking part of the wave and coming down with it

glassy: when there is no wind to ripple the wave face

gnarly: awesome

goofy foot: a surfer who rides waves with the right leg forward

grommet or grom: a young surfer

kick out: to thrust out of the wave at the end of the ride

lineup: the spot in the ocean where surfers get in line to catch waves, just behind the breaking zone

off the top: a turn on the top of a wave

perfect 10: a perfectly ridden wave in competitive surfing

pop-up: the quick move a surfer makes to rise to a standing position when taking off on a wave

pump: an up-and-down carving movement to generate speed

set: a group of waves

skunked: having no good waves to surf

slash or snap: a rapid turn off the top of a wave

soup: the broken foam of a wave

stoked: enthusiastic or excited about something

trough: the bottom of the wave

tube riding (or "getting barreled"): riding through the hollow curl of a wave

ABOUT WAVE REPORTS

Calculations and measurements that report wind, wave, tide, swell, air, and water conditions

Wind: how fast and from what direction the air is blowing. But be aware, wind can change throughout the day.

Q. *Why does wind matter?*

A. Onshore winds, the kind that blow from the ocean toward land, often cause choppy water. In other words, not so great surfing conditions. But offshore winds, which blow from land out to sea, can delay the breaking of a wave. This makes it steeper and more

powerful, and may give Bethany the
opportunity to get tubed—or ride deep inside
a wave.

Wave height: the height, measured in feet, from
the peak—or top—of a wave to its trough—
or its lowest point

Wave period: waves come in sets; a wave period
is how many seconds pass between each
wave within that set.

Q. Why do the wave height and period matter?

A. Because Bethany wants to ride a powerful
wave! And the longer a wave's period, the
more power it will have when it breaks.

Tide direction: the direction the water flows as the tide comes in—or rises—and goes out—or falls

Q. **Why does the tide direction matter?**

A. Rising and falling tides can affect rip currents and wave consistency. Surf spots vary. One can be great during low tide, while another could leave Bethany skunked.

Swell direction: the direction a swell—or the waves out in the ocean—are coming from, such as a SW (southwest) swell

Q. **Why does the swell direction matter?**

A. Like the other factors, a good swell could mean the difference between Bethany **getting barreled** or staring at glassy water, hoping the wind changes. If a swell rolls in from the south, then a beach facing north may have nothing but flat water.

Air and water temperature: measured in degrees, how warm or cold the air and water is

Q. *Why does the temperature matter?*

A. For Bethany, in the warm waters of Hawaii, it doesn't matter too much. But for surfers around the world, they may need to grab a wet suit if the water is cold.

RECOMMENDED READING

Soul Surfer: A True Story of Faith, Family, and Fighting to Get Back on the Board by Bethany Hamilton and Rick Bundschuh with Sheryl Berk

Be Unstoppable: The Art of Never Giving Up by Bethany Hamilton

I Survived the Shark Attacks of 1916 by Lauren Tarshis

Shark Attack! by Cathy East Dubowski

Storm Surfer by Jake Maddox

BIBLIOGRAPHY

Books, Articles, TV, and Film

"Bethany Hamilton & Cold Mountain." *20/20*, season 25, episode 6. ABC TV, November 21, 2003.

Hamilton, Bethany, with Dorris Rikkers. *Ask Bethany: FAQs: Surfing, Faith & Friends*. Grand Rapids, MI: Zonderkidz, 2011.

Hamilton, Bethany, and Rick Bundschuh, with
    Sheryl Berk. *Soul Surfer: A True Story of
    Faith, Family, and Fighting to Get Back on the
    Board*. New York: Pocket Books, 2004.

*Heart of a Soul Surfer: The Bethany Hamilton
    Documentary*. Directed by Becky
    Baumgartner. Friends of Bethany, Walking
    on Water, and Shankly Productions, 2007.

"Surfer Girl Makes Comeback after Shark
    Attack." ABC News, April 7, 2005. Accessed
    October 29, 2016, http://abcnews.go.com
    /Primetime/Health/story?id=644247.

Websites

"2004 NSSA National Championships—The
Greatest Show on Earth." NSSA website,
July 1, 2004, accessed October 30, 2016,
http://www.nssa.org/newsmanager
/templates/NSSAArticle.aspx?articleid=6.

Bethany Hamilton, accessed September 29, 2016,
http://bethanyhamilton.com.

"Shark Attack Facts," accessed April 26, 2017,
http://natgeotv.com/ca/human-shark-bait
/facts.

"Shark Identification Guide," accessed July 26,
2016, http://dlnr.hawaii.gov/sharks/hawaii
-sharks/shark-identification-guide.

ABOUT THE AUTHOR

Photo by April Ziegler

JENNI L. WALSH spent a decade enticing readers as an award-winning advertising copywriter before becoming an author. Now her passion lies in transporting readers to another world, be it in historical or contemporary settings. She is a proud graduate of Villanova University and lives in the Philadelphia suburbs with her husband, daughter, son, and newfypoo. She also writes historical fiction for adults and children. Learn more about Jenni and her books at jennilwalsh.com.

Read about more girls who dared!

Don't miss:

Meet Malala. Get inspired.